TO ROB, THE NUMBER ONE FAN OF THIS SERIES
(BESIDES THE NATIONAL)

Published by
Princeton Architectural Press
A division of Chronicle Books LLC
70 West 36th Street
New York, NY 10018
www.papress.com

Published by arrangement with Debbie Bibo Agency

ISBN 978-1-7972-2243-1

Designer: Camilla Pintonato
Translation: Sylvia Notini

For Princeton Architectural Press:
Editors: Kristen Hewitt, Rob Shaeffer
Typesetting: Natalie Snodgrass

Library of Congress Cataloging-in-Publication Data
Names: Demonti, Ilaria, author. | Pintonato, Camilla, illustrator.
Title: Sheepology : the ultimate encyclopedia / Ilaria Demonti, Camilla
    Pintonato.
Description: New York, NY : Princeton Architectural Press, [2022] |
Audience: Ages 6 - 10 | Audience: Grades 2-3 | Summary: "Discover all
    there is to know about sheep in all of their woolly mammal glory in
    Sheepology"-- Provided by publisher.
Identifiers: LCCN 2022026591 | ISBN 9781797222431 (hardcover) | ISBN
    9781797224190 (ebook)
Subjects: LCSH: Sheep--Juvenile literature.
Classification: LCC SF375.2 .D48 2022 | DDC 636.3--dc23/eng/20220711
LC record available at https://lccn.loc.gov/2022026591

ILARIA DEMONTI   CAMILLA PINTONATO

SHEEPOLOGY
THE ULTIMATE ENCYCLOPEDIA

PA PRESS

PRINCETON ARCHITECTURAL PRESS · NEW YORK

CONTENTS

MEET THE FLOCK

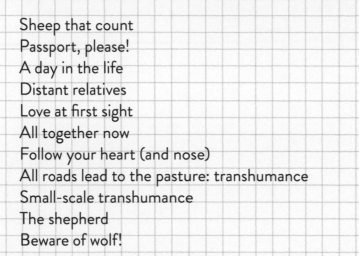

WHAT ARE SHEEP LIKE?

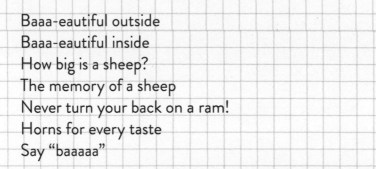

MILK
AND WOOL

HUMANS AND SHEEP
LIVING TOGETHER

SHEEP BREEDS

SHEEP THAT COUNT

Our lives wouldn't be the same without sheep. We owe a great deal to this tame and docile animal that over thousands of years has nourished us with its milk and its cheese, kept us warm with its wool—allowing us to survive in the coldest environments—and accompanied us to every corner of the planet.

Today, if we really wanted to count ALL the sheep in the world before falling asleep, we would have to count to 1.2 billion: around one sheep for every six people. But the success of sheep goes way back.

Along with the goat, it was among the first herbivores to be domesticated by humans, allowing us to develop a sedentary lifestyle. Later, sheep would supply raw material for the flourishing wool trade.

Owning sheep has historically been synonymous with wealth, which is why this animal has been celebrated in various religions and cultures where it often has an important symbolic meaning.

PASSPORT, PLEASE!

All sheep are not the same: they come in different breeds, sizes, and colors. There are long-, medium-, and short-haired sheep. There are sheep with lots of wool and sheep with no wool at all, as well as sheep that shed their wool without needing to be sheared. Their faces can be black, white, or red; they can have up to six horns, or none at all; and they can have a tail…or not! And yet, they all belong to a single large flock that has flourished throughout the whole world.

THE SHEEP

FACE	A sheep's face can be black, white, or red.
HORNS	Sheep can have anywhere from zero to six horns.
TAIL	Some sheep have one, others do not.
FLEECE	This varies in color and length.

HOOVES

The sheep is an artiodactyl, which means it has an even number of functional toes on each foot. Its front legs are supported by the top of the middle toes.

HERBIVOROUS

The sheep is an herbivore—that is, it eats only grass, and it is a ruminant, meaning its stomach is divided into four separate stomach compartments where the food is digested in a long and laborious process, after which it is sent back to the mouth to be chewed a second time.

BOVID

The sheep belongs to the family of Bovidae together with other domestic animals like the cow, the buffalo, and the goat, and also wild animals like the Alpine ibex, gazelles, and goat-antelopes.

MAMMAL

The mothers nurse their young.

A DAY IN THE LIFE OF A SHEEP

Who says it's better to spend one day as a lion than one hundred years as a sheep? The typical day of a sheep is nothing to sneeze at!

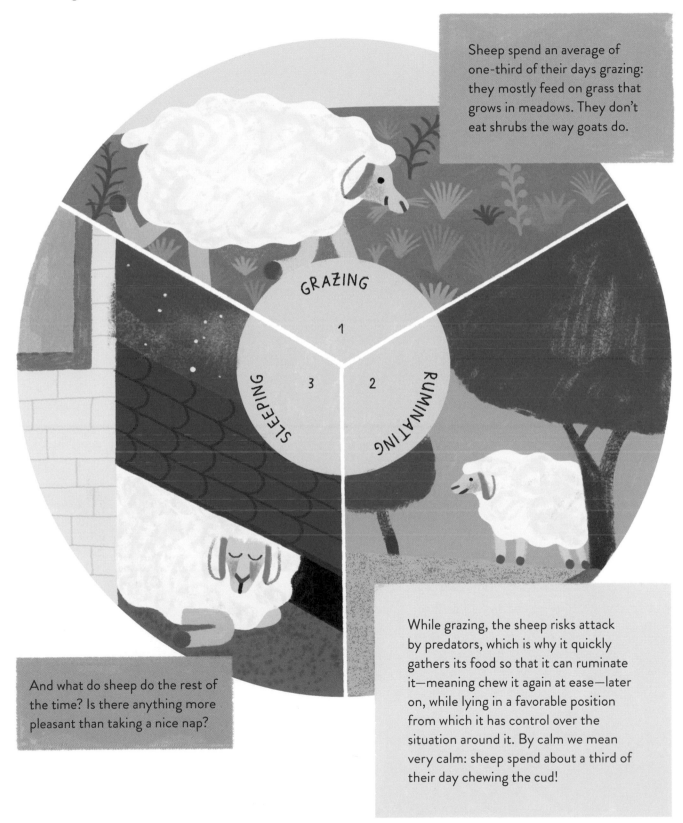

Sheep spend an average of one-third of their days grazing: they mostly feed on grass that grows in meadows. They don't eat shrubs the way goats do.

GRAZING
1

RUMINATING
2

SLEEPING
3

And what do sheep do the rest of the time? Is there anything more pleasant than taking a nice nap?

While grazing, the sheep risks attack by predators, which is why it quickly gathers its food so that it can ruminate it—meaning chew it again at ease—later on, while lying in a favorable position from which it has control over the situation around it. By calm we mean very calm: sheep spend about a third of their day chewing the cud!

DISTANT RELATIVES

The docile sheep we see grazing peacefully in meadows seem to have nothing in common with their wild ancestors. To adapt to the climates of their new environments, and thanks to the crossbreeding carried out by humans, little by little sheep began to change, eventually becoming the animals we are familiar with today.

Wild sheep are not sheared: they have long, coarse hair that covers a soft undercoat of wool on their skin that they shed in spring.

They are predominantly brown, often with a darker back and a lighter stomach, and they have a shorter tail.

Male sheep have large, curved horns that they use to fight each other, butting heads to impose their domination over the group. In most breeds, female sheep also have horns.

In many domestic breeds, neither the males nor the females have horns.

Domestic sheep have stockier legs.

Domesticated sheep that are bred for their wool have finer hair and more wool, which never stops growing and must be sheared regularly. Humans tend to breed sheep with a white fleece, which is easier to dye.

12

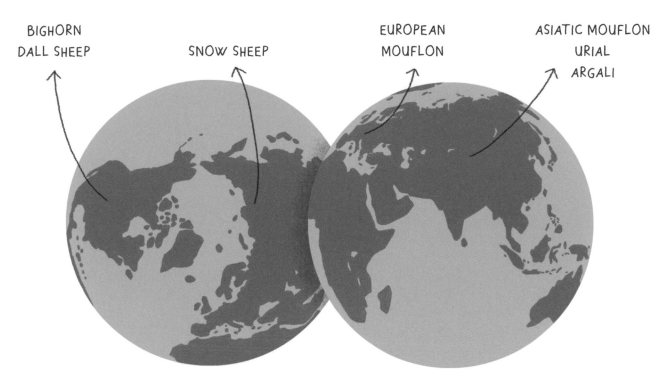

BIGHORN
DALL SHEEP

SNOW SHEEP

EUROPEAN
MOUFLON

ASIATIC MOUFLON
URIAL
ARGALI

The ancestors of sheep took their first steps at high altitudes, in the mountains of Central Asia, between 10 and 20 million years ago. During the last glacial period some of them migrated east, toward Siberia, and even crossed the Bering Strait, reaching North America, where they were never domesticated. In Siberia, western North America, northern Canada, and Alaska you can still meet the wild sheep that directly descend from these adventurous "pioneer" sheep.

The ancestors of modern domesticated sheep instead migrated west across Asia and toward Europe: it isn't easy to find the roots of this complicated animal family tree, but it is likely that our domestic sheep descended from the Asiatic mouflon.

Some of the wild descendants of the first sheep, which are very different from domesticated sheep, can still be found today in some corners of Europe and Asia.

LOVE AT FIRST SIGHT

Sheep have accompanied humans since the dawn of time. While at first our ancestors hunted wild sheep for their meat, as the millennia passed, the domestication of wild sheep helped allow migrating cultures to transition to a sedentary life, and things changed rapidly. About 11,000 years ago in the Middle East agriculture began to spread, and likely as early 9,000 years ago animals that lived in flocks began to be domesticated instead of hunted.

SUPER MANURE

Thanks to sheep manure the uncultivated land where these animals graze is fertile. Bringing a flock of sheep to a field that needs to be cultivated is still the easiest way to get it ready to farm. Manure was also historically used to line huts, and even today in many communities it is still used as a fuel for heating and cooking, in the form of dung.

Soon sheep began to be bred for their milk as well: the oldest piece of cheese discovered by archaeologists is dated to 7,200 years ago!

Only later did humans learn to use and work sheep's wool. Although the first wool textiles have not survived, the earliest traces that have been preserved are more than 5,000 years old.

ALL TOGETHER NOW

Sheep don't like to be alone. They're social animals, which means they love company. And they're docile animals that have no problem living all together in large flocks, welcoming other breeds of sheep, and even other animals, with which they live peacefully.

HUDDLED TOGETHER

Strength through unity! Sheep know that if they stay close together, they're more likely to survive the attacks of predators.

BEEEEEHH!

BEEEEEEHH!

BAA?

Sheep baa, or bleat, but the sound they make differs depending on the situation: for example, when a mother addresses her baby, or when a male wants his mate to hear him, the sounds they make are distinctive. And they snort when they're nervous, uncomfortable, or frightened.

BEEEEEEEEEEHHH

16

EWE

A ewe is an adult female that has given birth at least once.

An adult male sheep is called a ram. Although sheep are docile, sometimes rams will fight each other to establish their role in the flock.

RAM

WEANED LAMB

Male and female lambs are weaned between three and eight months of age.

A suckling lamb is less than one month old and hasn't been weaned yet.

SUCKLING LAMB

LAMB

Baby sheep are called lambs until they can make their own babies, which generally happens by their first birthday.

FOLLOW YOUR HEART (AND NOSE)

Tell me what you smell like, and I'll tell you who you are. Thanks to their sense of smell, sheep can tell who is and who isn't a member of their flock, they can establish the hierarchy between males and females, and they can launch signals of seduction during courtship. And every lamb has a unique smell that its mother uses to recognize it. She would never mistake it for any other lamb.

I LIKE YOUR SMELL

As for courtship, it's the females that take the lead. Starting from seven to eight months of age, they use their irresistible smell to attract the rams. The most popular males, who mate with the highest number of females, are the dominant ones.

A MATTER OF FEELING

Before they mate, the ewe and the ram follow each other around in a circle, taking turns sniffing each other. Often, the male is so excited he wets himself, while the female remains motionless, turning her head to one side.

THE RAM'S ACE UP THE SLEEVE

As a ram chooses its mate, his face has a strange smile—it is hard to know if it's because the ram is flattered, incredibly happy, or just plain foolish. He curls back his upper lip and shows his toothless grin, while proudly lifting his head. This is called the flehmen response, a behavior that helps sheep and other animals receive the scents of pheromones, chemical messages linked to mating.

PREGNANCY AND BIRTH

After five months of pregnancy, sheep give birth to one lamb at a time, but they can have twins or even triplets. On the day the ewe is ready to give birth, she looks for a quiet place where she can bring to light her tiny offspring. Lambing is quick: it takes place in less than an hour.

HUDDLED TOGETHER

The mama sheep stays with her little one, licking it to remove the traces of placenta and keep it warm, feeding it milk just like a human mother with her child.

ATTENTION!

It takes only ten to twenty minutes after birth for a lamb to stand, and only a few hours to walk, run, and jump. It instantly seeks its mother's nipple: nursing during the first days of life is essential to the little one's growth.

LITTLE LAMBS GROW UP

After a few days, the ewe and the lamb join the flocks, never separating from each other. In time the lamb wanders farther and farther away, but it's always within hearing range of its mother's bleating so that it can find her right away when it's time to nurse again. By the time it's four months old, the lamb learns to feed itself, leaving the sheep free to be milked by the shepherd.

ALL ROADS LEAD TO THE PASTURE: TRANSHUMANCE

In the lowlands, when it gets really hot and the sun scorches the grass, the shepherd leads his flock of sheep in search of greener pastures. This seasonal migration between grazing areas is known as transhumance, but unfortunately today the tradition is vanishing. It was once a legendary practice that happened throughout the world.

COMMUTER LIFE

Transhumance occurred over vast distances for long periods of time across Asia and Europe. Flocks would spend seven months in the lowlands, from November to May, and five months in the mountains, from June to October.

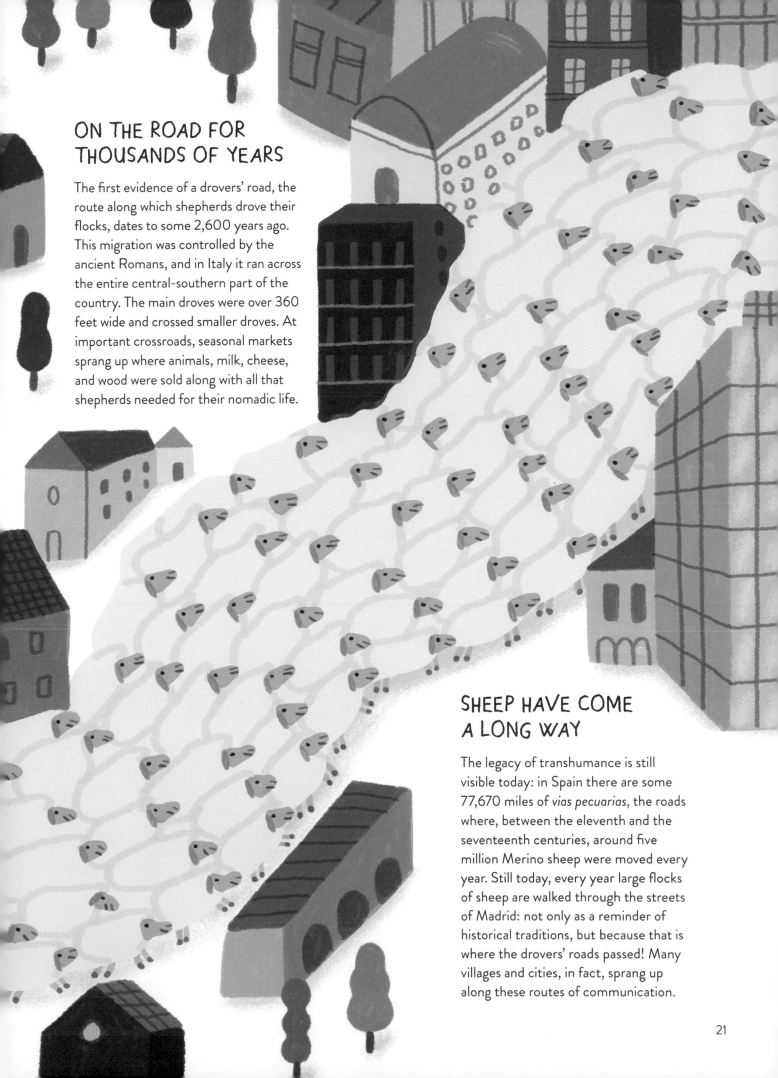

ON THE ROAD FOR THOUSANDS OF YEARS

The first evidence of a drovers' road, the route along which shepherds drove their flocks, dates to some 2,600 years ago. This migration was controlled by the ancient Romans, and in Italy it ran across the entire central-southern part of the country. The main droves were over 360 feet wide and crossed smaller droves. At important crossroads, seasonal markets sprang up where animals, milk, cheese, and wood were sold along with all that shepherds needed for their nomadic life.

SHEEP HAVE COME A LONG WAY

The legacy of transhumance is still visible today: in Spain there are some 77,670 miles of *vias pecuarias*, the roads where, between the eleventh and the seventeenth centuries, around five million Merino sheep were moved every year. Still today, every year large flocks of sheep are walked through the streets of Madrid: not only as a reminder of historical traditions, but because that is where the drovers' roads passed! Many villages and cities, in fact, sprang up along these routes of communication.

SMALL-SCALE TRANSHUMANCE

One type of transhumance still takes place today in the Alps: it is repeated every year from the lowlands to the pastures in the spring, and back down again in the fall. Traditionally, shearing takes place after transhumance: shearing in September is also a way to celebrate the shepherds' return to their native villages.

Often shepherds and their animals were not looked upon kindly by farmers, who feared that the flocks crossing their land would damage their crops.

WALK THIS WAY

When one sheep starts moving, all the others will follow. Shepherds will exploit this behavior to guide the flock.

THE LAMBS

Most of the time today the animals are transported in trucks, but Alpine transhumance can also take place on foot just as it once did, and can last from ten to twenty days. The trek is too long and wearisome for the lambs, and they are often transported on a donkey's back.

THE SHEPHERD

Being a shepherd is one of the toughest jobs in the world. The shepherd's job is to care for and protect the sheep by taking them out to pasture, finding them shelter, and milking and shearing them.

ALGERIA

MONGOLIA

INDIA

THE SHEEPDOG

Every shepherd needs a dog: there are dogs that are faithful to their master and help to keep the flock together, chasing after any sheep that gets lost along the way. There are also guard dogs that will defend the flock from predators at all costs.

BANKHAR DOG

BORDER COLLIE

24

Originally, shepherds were nomads and lived in tribal groups that were constantly on the move from one pasture to another, depending on their animals for their survival. This practice is still widespread in Tibet, among the Bedouins of the Middle Eastern desert, and in Mongolia, where seminomadic shepherds make up a quarter of the population. Nowadays, the roaming flock is becoming less common.

NEPAL

AFGHANISTAN

ITALY

GERMAN SHEPHERD

HUNGARIAN PULI

A PRESTIGIOUS JOB

The image of the shepherd has been held in great esteem by many cultures from ancient times: King Hammurabi of Babylon described himself as "the shepherd who brings peace," and in the Jewish, Christian, and Muslim religions God is often referred to as "the good shepherd."

BEWARE OF WOLF!

Although the docile nature of sheep makes it easy to breed them, it also leaves them more vulnerable to the attacks of numerous meat-eating predators. Since domestic sheep don't have horns, nor the large bulk that cows have, nor any way of taking shelter in a safe place like a henhouse the way chickens can, when sheep are grazing, their only means of defense is to stay together in the flock or make a run for it. But over the years the number of predators in the wild has diminished, and such attacks are less frequent than they once were.

SHEEP

Besides building fences and keeping sheep in pens, a good strategy to protect them is to provide a livestock guardian: for thousands of years humans have used shepherding dogs to tend flocks. Nowadays sheep are also entrusted to the protection of donkeys, whose braying, biting, and powerful kicking can scare off even a wolf. Sometimes llamas are used, since they're perfect for keeping small predators at bay.

DONKEY

LLAMA

SHEPHERD DOG

In the United States, the sheep's greatest enemy is the coyote, a distant relative of the dog and the wolf.

The wolf is no doubt the most notorious enemy of sheep. Everyone knows Aesop's fable "The Boy Who Cried Wolf."

COYOTE

WOLF

FOX

LYNX

BEAR

Stray dogs can also be a danger to sheep.

Because birds of prey are small, they don't often attack sheep. But when a golden eagle flies over a flock, better watch out!

STRAY DOG

BIRD OF PREY

TEAM 2

BAAA-EAUTIFUL OUTSIDE

TAIL

A sheep's tail protects the anus and the genitals, is used
to swat flies, and is even used to communicate.
Some sheep breeds living in the warmest
countries accumulate fat in this part
of the body, on the buttocks
and the back.

FLEECE

The feature that the domestic sheep is most famous for is
its fleece, or fur, made up of fine curly hair or wool. This is
distinct from coarser, prickly, and sparse hair that still grows
on some sheep breeds, though it has almost disappeared
from others. The fleece must be shorn regularly because it
never stops growing. Take Chris, an unfortunate Australian
Merino ram, who somehow got separated from his flock and
turned into a gigantic ball of wool. When Chris was finally
found five years later, a record amount of wool was shorn
from him: over eighty-eight pounds!

HOOVES

Sheep instinctively remain perfectly still
when they're lifted, and their hooves
don't touch the ground. Shepherds take
advantage of this behavior for shearing by
rolling the sheep over onto their backs. The
sheep then can't get up without help, so
they can be sheared easily!

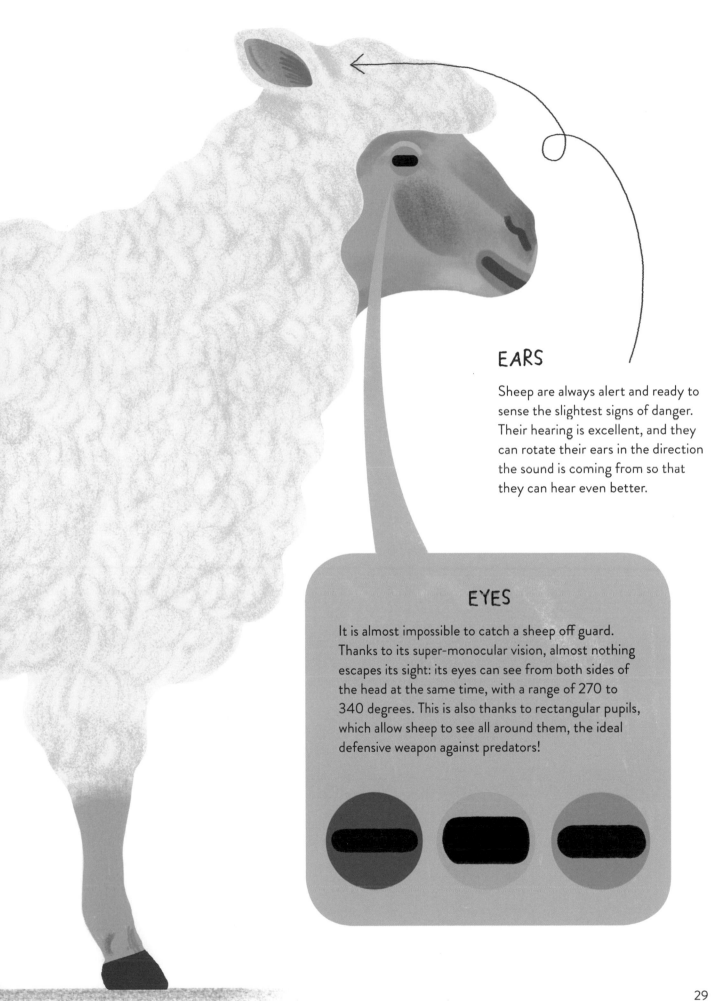

EARS

Sheep are always alert and ready to sense the slightest signs of danger. Their hearing is excellent, and they can rotate their ears in the direction the sound is coming from so that they can hear even better.

EYES

It is almost impossible to catch a sheep off guard. Thanks to its super-monocular vision, almost nothing escapes its sight: its eyes can see from both sides of the head at the same time, with a range of 270 to 340 degrees. This is also thanks to rectangular pupils, which allow sheep to see all around them, the ideal defensive weapon against predators!

BAAA-EAUTIFUL INSIDE

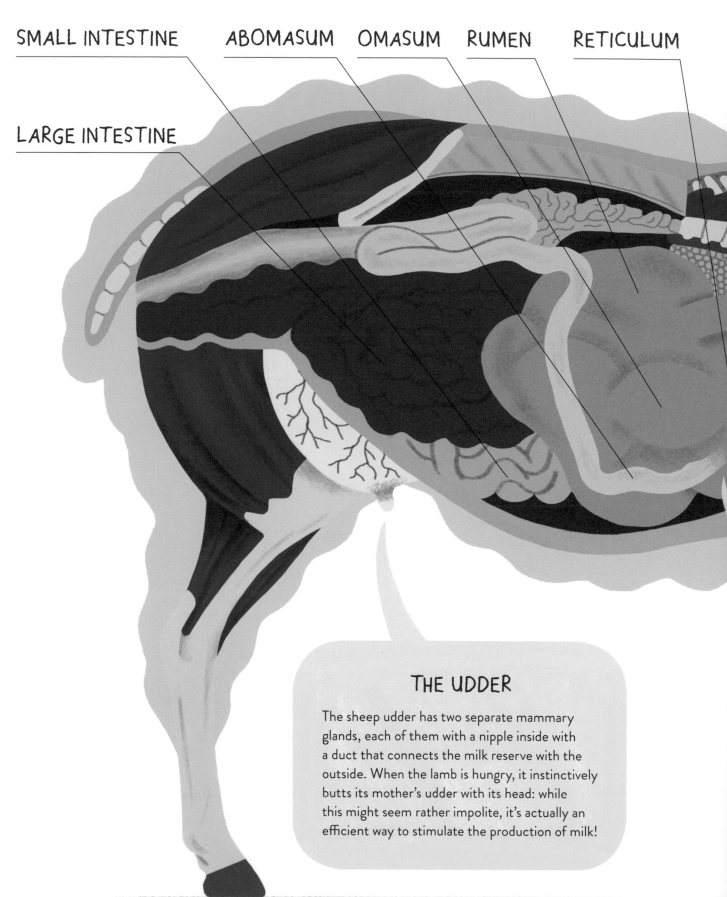

SMALL INTESTINE ABOMASUM OMASUM RUMEN RETICULUM

LARGE INTESTINE

THE UDDER

The sheep udder has two separate mammary glands, each of them with a nipple inside with a duct that connects the milk reserve with the outside. When the lamb is hungry, it instinctively butts its mother's udder with its head: while this might seem rather impolite, it's actually an efficient way to stimulate the production of milk!

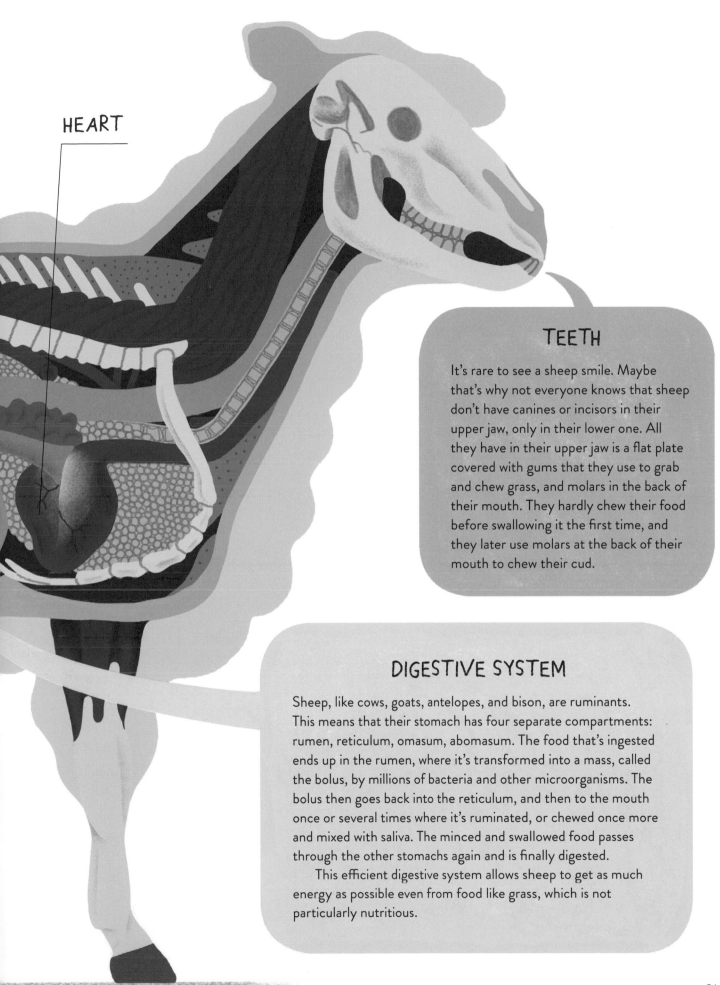

HEART

TEETH

It's rare to see a sheep smile. Maybe that's why not everyone knows that sheep don't have canines or incisors in their upper jaw, only in their lower one. All they have in their upper jaw is a flat plate covered with gums that they use to grab and chew grass, and molars in the back of their mouth. They hardly chew their food before swallowing it the first time, and they later use molars at the back of their mouth to chew their cud.

DIGESTIVE SYSTEM

Sheep, like cows, goats, antelopes, and bison, are ruminants. This means that their stomach has four separate compartments: rumen, reticulum, omasum, abomasum. The food that's ingested ends up in the rumen, where it's transformed into a mass, called the bolus, by millions of bacteria and other microorganisms. The bolus then goes back into the reticulum, and then to the mouth once or several times where it's ruminated, or chewed once more and mixed with saliva. The minced and swallowed food passes through the other stomachs again and is finally digested.

This efficient digestive system allows sheep to get as much energy as possible even from food like grass, which is not particularly nutritious.

HOW BIG IS A SHEEP?

Sheep come in all sizes: the biggest wild sheep is the Argali, while among domestic sheep the Suffolk Stratford Whisperer H23 ram is the biggest—it made it into the Guinness World Records by surpassing the Lincoln sheep, which is on average very large. The smallest sheep is the French Ouessant, which is more or less the size of a poodle.

OUESSANT
AROUND 20
INCHES

BABYDOLL
AROUND 23
INCHES

LINCOLN
AROUND 35
INCHES

SUFFOLK
AROUND 42
INCHES

ARGALI
AROUND 50
INCHES

THE MEMORY OF A SHEEP

Who says sheep are brainless? Their gregarious and docile behavior might lead one to believe that sheep are not intelligent animals, but countless experiments have shown that quite the opposite is true.

GUESS WHO?

Sheep have an excellent memory for faces: show them fifty different ones and they'll remember them all, even after two years have passed!

And not just that: they can distinguish a smiling face from a scowling one. How was this discovery made? By placing two pictures on two doors that had to be crossed in order to get a snack. The sheep always chose the door with the happy face.

Sheep can easily get their bearings in a maze, quickly learning and memorizing the fastest way to join the flock waiting for them at the exit.

Necessity is the mother of invention: to overcome the obstacles that prevented them from roaming around the village as they pleased, some English sheep learned to simply roll over barriers. A full-scale military operation.

35

NEVER TURN YOUR BACK ON A RAM!

To earn the right to reproduce, rams fight by butting heads. Bighorn wild sheep males can fight for twenty-four hours straight. These animals have massive horns that weigh thirty pounds, and a reinforced skull connected to the vertebral column by a thick ligament. Talk about hard-headed!

Even the males who might seem docile can suddenly headbutt another ram when least expected.

HORNS FOR EVERY TASTE

While wild sheep can boast of large horns used for defense or competition, not all domestic sheep have them. In some breeds only the ram has them, while in others both males and females may either have them or not. Male horns are generally larger than female horns, varying in shape and number from breed to breed.

A MATTER OF STYLE

While most domestic sheep don't have horns, there are some exceptions to the rule: the Jacob sheep, for example, can have from two to four horns, and in some cases as many as six!

1. Ram with curved horns
2. Female sheep with horns
3. Ram with spiral horns
4. Undeveloped horns
5. Jacob four-horn sheep

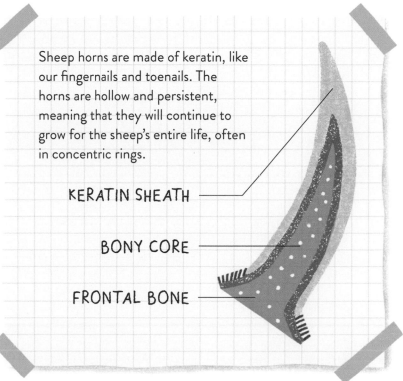

Sheep horns are made of keratin, like our fingernails and toenails. The horns are hollow and persistent, meaning that they will continue to grow for the sheep's entire life, often in concentric rings.

KERATIN SHEATH

BONY CORE

FRONTAL BONE

1

2

3

4

5

SAY "BAAAAA"

To keep the flock healthy, the sheep must be fed a proper diet and given the right amount of space. Their hygiene and any illnesses should be taken care of with the help of a veterinarian. Here are some of the most common illnesses among sheep:

ECHINOCOCCOSIS

This disease is caused by the tapeworm, a dangerous parasite that can affect mammals, including humans.

MANGE

Caused by parasitic mites that can either colonize the surface of the skin or burrow through it; symptoms include itching and loss of wool.

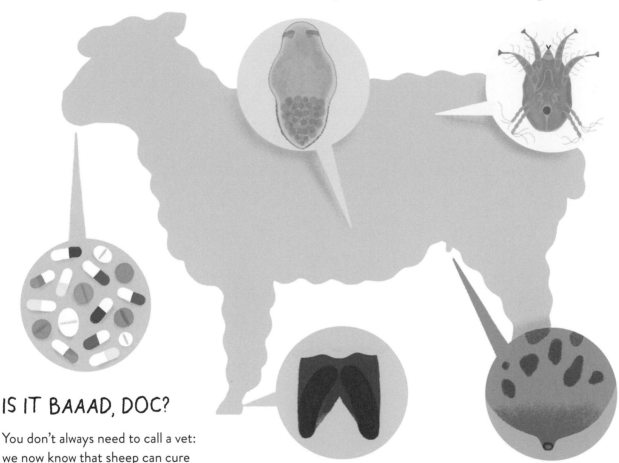

IS IT BAAAD, DOC?

You don't always need to call a vet: we now know that sheep can cure themselves of certain diseases. During an experiment, after they were treated a first time by a human, some of the lambs knew exactly which food they needed to treat a mild case of malaise. Not bad for an animal that's considered unintelligent!

FOOT DISEASE

Foot disease affects the sheep's hoof, causing it to limp.

MASTITIS

This common disease affects the sheep's udder, which becomes warm to the touch, reddish-blue, and painful. If discovered in time, however, it can easily be treated.

AM I SEEING DOUBLE?

Dolly is one of the most famous sheep in the world, the first mammal cloned from an adult cell. Dolly, in other words, was an exact copy of another sheep with which she shared the same genetic composition, instead of only half, as is the case with natural reproduction.

Created in 1996 in a lab near Edinburgh, after some 276 failed attempts, Dolly showed that animals can be cloned from any cell and not just from embryo or stem cells. This discovery aroused a great deal of ethical debate: Is it right to clone an animal? Is the cloning of a sheep the first step toward the cloning of a human being? What are the limits of science?

SHEEP'S MILK

All mammals feed their newborns with their own milk, an exceptional source of nutrition that contains fundamental beneficial substances for growth. But adult humans often continue to drink the milk of other animals, especially cow's milk. Although it mainly consists of water, a glass of milk is more nourishing than a plate of spaghetti: it has fewer calories but is rich in vitamins and mineral salts, which are important for our health.

SMELL

The strong smell of sheep's milk is a result of the grazing of the flock: the flavor and smells of the grass can transfer into their milk. This means that each region's sheep's milk has its own unique smell.

ON THE SHELF

Even though today cow's milk predominates in supermarkets and on the table, the sheep was the first animal to be milked by humans. But people drink many other types of milk around the world, from goats, donkeys, buffalo, and camels.

MILK-PRODUCING SHEEP

All sheep can be milked, but certain breeds produce more milk than others and are selected and bred for this reason. The breed that produces the most milk in the world is the Friesian, which can make as much as five pounds of milk per day, almost twice the average of the other breeds!

5 LBS

WHAT DOES A DROP OF SHEEP'S MILK CONSIST OF?

VITAMINS AND MINERAL SALTS

around 1%

With respect to other types of milk, sheep's milk contains more of vitamins A, B, and E, as well as calcium, phosphorus, and magnesium.

WATER

around 81%

FATS AND PROTEIN

fats around 7%, protein around 6%

Sheep's milk is much richer in fats and protein than the milk of other animals: this is why it isn't easy to drink a whole glass, which is best used to make cheese.

LACTOSE

around 5%

Lactose is a type of sugar. For it to be digested, it requires an enzyme that humans may stop producing as they grow: people who are lactose intolerant can't drink milk.

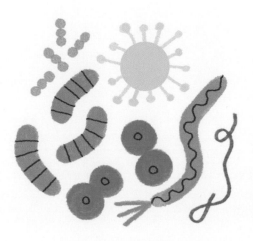

BEST IF PASTEURIZED

In addition to these elements, milk also contains microorganisms that are dangerous to our health: that's why milk must be pasteurized before it's sold. Pasteurized milk, or milk that has been heated from 145 to 176 degrees Fahrenheit, is both safe and can be preserved longer.

HOW IS CHEESE MADE?

To make cheese, you need only three ingredients: milk, rennet, and salt. And yet in today's world there are over two thousand types of cheese, which vary in shape, color, and flavor. And these include hundreds of sheep's milk cheeses. By changing just a few of the steps, you get a completely different type of cheese.

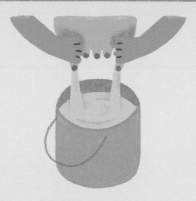

MILKING

You get the milk by milking the sheep. On small farms this is still done by hand, but on bigger ones, automatic milking machines are used.

CURDLING

Filtered milk is heated to 91–98 degrees Fahrenheit and rennet is added, a substance that separates fats and proteins from the watery part known as whey.

CUTTING THE CURDS

When the right consistency has been reached, the next step is cutting the curds into lots of smaller ones. Their size will determine the consistency of the cheese. By reheating the curds, you can make other types of cheese.

SHAPING

The curds are placed inside special molds and pressed to remove any remaining liquid.

SALTING

Salt is a preservative, and, besides enhancing the flavor, it also prevents the cheese from spoiling. It can be added directly to the curd, or it can be rubbed on the outside of the wheel of cheese.

RIPENING

The last step is the ripening. That's when the cheese is allowed to age. This can take just a few days for soft cheeses to several years for the harder ones.

POLYPHEMUS

The history of sheep's milk cheese is almost legendary: the *Odyssey* tells the story of when Odysseus entered the cave of the cyclops Polyphemus. There Odysseus found several wheels of sheep's milk cheese, as well as the various pieces of equipment used by the dairyman, also known as a cheesemaker.

EXTRACTION OF THE CURDS

After the curds have been broken up, they are separated from the whey. The whey is then heated up a second time at about 176 degrees Fahrenheit to make ricotta cheese.

IT'S DINNER TIME!

Sheep's milk cheese can be eaten in lots of different ways, and it's the main ingredient in many delicious recipes all around the world.

CHEESEOLOGY

To make cheese, you can use milk from a cow, goat, buffalo, or even a horse, llama, or yak. Have you ever tasted cheese made with sheep's milk? There are different types of sheep's milk cheese, but its strong, almost wild taste is unmistakable whatever the type of cheese may be.

1

2

3

4

5

6

ROQUEFORT
1996

PAPIL

1. MANCHEGO

This high-quality cheese is rigorously produced with the milk of sheep bred in the Castilla–La Mancha region in the heart of Spain.

2. PECORINO ROMANO

Pecorino has been around almost 2,000 years, and the type we eat today isn't very different from the one that was made by the ancient Romans.

3. HALLOUMI

Brought to Cyprus by the Arabs, halloumi was embraced by both Greek and Turkish cuisine and has become one of the most widespread cheeses in the world.

4. FETA

In Homer's *Odyssey*, Polyphemus the Cyclops made feta in his cave. It was probably one of the first cheeses made by humans and is still today one of the most beloved and famous in the world: feta is the national cheese of Greece.

5. SHANKLISH

Produced on the border of Lebanon and Syria, this cheese, with its pungent flavor, traditionally was eaten for breakfast by Lebanese shepherds.

6. ROQUEFORT

Which ingredient makes "the cheese of kings and popes" so delicious? Hard to believe it's mold!

7. TUSHURI GUDA

The "guda" is a sheepskin sack that's turned inside out and used to store the cheese that's named for it. This method of cheesemaking is an ancient Georgian tradition that has 6,000 years of history.

8. OSCYPEK

As beautiful as it is tasty, this smoked cheese from Poland is poured into wooden molds made from the plantain tree. In the past the molds were decorated by shepherds.

9. QAREHQURUT

Though it looks like candy, it's actually dried cheese that's used in many recipes in Persian and Middle Eastern cuisine.

SHEEP'S MILK CHEESE IN WORLD CUISINE

Sheep's milk cheese was probably the first kind of cheese made by humans. Whether it originated in Europe, Central Asia, or the Middle East, where it's used in many recipes, is still unknown. The use of sheep's milk cheese is less widespread in the culinary traditions of North and South America and Asia, where it arrived "only" a few centuries ago.

CUAJADA

GRILLED (SHEEP) CHEESE SANDWICH

SPAIN

USA

CACIO E PEPE

ITALY

CYPRUS

PALESTINE

GREECE

GREEK SALAD

FRIED HALLOUMI

KNAFEH NABULSEYEH

ROQUEFORT FILET MIGNON

GRILLED OSCYPEK WITH ŻURAWINA (CRANBERRY) JAM

BRYNDZOVÉ HALUŠKY

FRANCE

POLAND

SLOVAKIA

BULGARIA

BANITSA

MONGOLIA

AARUUL

JORDAN

TURKEY

IRAN

AL-RASHOOF

STUFFED PITA

KASHKE BADEMJAN

47

A CLOSER LOOK AT THE FLEECE

Sheep always have just the right look: their fleece comes in different colors, from white to brown to black, from reddish to gray, and it's ideal for every season. The wool protects sheep from both hot and cold weather—one of the many special qualities of this precious fiber.

WOOL UNDER THE MICROSCOPE

Wool fibers are made of keratin, just like our hair, and have no core. They range from 1.6 inches to around 14 inches in length, but are very thin: their diameter is between 16 and 40 microns (smaller than a one-thousandth of an inch)!

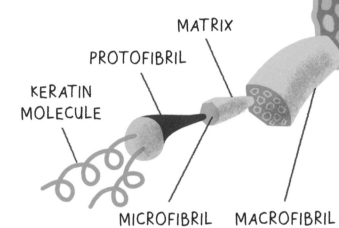

KERATIN MOLECULE

PROTOFIBRIL

MATRIX

MICROFIBRIL

MACROFIBRIL

CELL MEMBRANE COMPLEX

CORTEX

CUTICLE

LANOLIN

Secreted by the sebaceous glands in the skin, lanolin is the greasy wax that coats the fleece and protects it from the elements. Lanolin is collected by washing the wool in hot water and then skimming the grease off the surface. Humans continue to use it in many ways today: as a base for creams and medicines, to prevent rust, as a lubricant, in shoe polish, even to soften toilet paper.

TOILET PAPER

CREAM

ANTI-RUST

MILITARY UNIFORM

WOOL IS WATER REPELLENT

If you look at wool under a microscope, it looks a bit like a pine cone: it's covered in tiny scales that protect the fiber inside from water.

IT'S RESISTANT AND ELASTIC

IT'S FIRE-RESISTANT

Did you know that firefighters wear woolen underwear? Thanks to its high nitrogen and water content, wool burns at very high temperatures, 1,060 to 1,110 degrees Fahrenheit!

IT'S EASY TO DYE

Why? Because it absorbs color easily.

IT'S INSULATING

Air trapped between the fibers creates a thermal barrier: wool keeps you warm when it's chilly out, and cool when it's hot! Wool also creates an acoustic barrier, which is why it can be used to insulate a house.

TECHNICAL JACKET

TRENCH COAT

GABARDINE

In the mid-nineteenth century, Thomas Burberry discovered that lanolin had another amazing property: it could make the textiles it was applied to waterproof. Burberry thus invented and patented a new type of fabric known as gabardine, used to make classic, elegant outdoor coats, but also to waterproof military gear and even the clothes worn by explorers to the South Pole.

HANGING BY A THREAD

Some animals use their fur to protect themselves from the cold, while others are covered in feathers or scales. Humans do not have any such protection—instead they learned to make clothing to cover themselves: at first they used plant fibers, then, later, wool. The process has changed over the millennia, but those ancient processes continue to be used to make the sweaters and gloves we wear today.

BEFORE

WASHING

After sorting the various types of wool present in the fleece, it's time to do the washing. During this phase the wool releases lanolin in the water, which is then set aside.

CARDING

To disentangle the clumps of wool fibers, you need to card them by hand with sharp-toothed combs. Originally, thistles were used, prickly plants whose Latin name is *Carduus*, from which the name of the process is likely derived.

COMBING

To make sure that the yarn is of the highest quality, the carded wool must undergo another phase known as combing, which makes the yarn even smoother and softer by laying the fibers parallel to one another and removing the shorter ones.

SHEARING

Wool is shorn in the spring and sometimes in the fall too. Depending on its breed, genetics, and nutrition, a single sheep can produce between three and thirty-three pounds of grease wool, fleece that has not yet been cleaned and combed. While in the past, shearing was done with a special pair of scissors, called shears, today shepherds prefer electric shears, sort of like the razors used by barbers. One New Zealand shepherd entered the Guinness World Records for shearing some 495 sheep in just nine hours!

BAAAAAAA

AFTER

SPINNING

Spinning wool is almost like magic: the woolen fibers are twisted together to create a long and resistant thread. At one time it took a distaff and spindle to carry out the process, but today special machinery is used.

DYEING

The skeins of yarn that are the result of the spinning process are then steeped in dyebaths. Wool can be dyed with natural dyes from flowers and plants, the way our ancestors did, or with chemical dyes.

PROCESSING

Now that the yarn is ready, it can be used in many different ways. Have you ever tried making a woolen scarf? All you need are knitting needles or a crochet hook, a pattern, and lots of patience! Have fun!

HOW WOOL IS PROCESSED: FELT

Who was the first to figure out that by wetting and beating wool you could make felt? The origins of this simple technique, probably the first instance of processing of wool, are lost in legend. To make a simple version of felt at home, instead of using carded wool try starting with an old sweater.

158°F

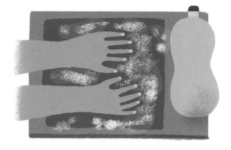

Take an old woolen sweater, maybe one that's already felted, and cut it up into several pieces starting from the sleeves.

Place the pieces of the sweater into very hot water, one at a time, gradually adding some liquid soap each time.

Rub the sweater on a flat surface for about one minute, then rinse in cold water.

After the material has dried, use scissors to cut the felt into squares of the same size or other shapes.

Sew the various patches together matching the colors as you like, until you get a rectangle.

Decorate the squares with other geometric shapes: now you have your first felt creation!

AN EMPIRE OF FELT

During the thirteenth century, Genghis Khan commanded his vast empire from a yurt, a tent made of felt that was used by the nomadic Mongols. The yurt was ideally suited for warfare because it was light and easy to move, but at the same time warm, waterproof, and sturdy. Thanks to the victories won with the help of the yurts, today it is estimated that one in every two hundred men alive is directly related to Genghis Khan!

HOW WOOL FABRIC IS MADE: KNITTING

All you need to knit is a ball of yarn and two knitting needles. It's a simple technique that anyone can learn and that is often taught in school because it helps kids stay focused and learn math in a practical way. At the same time, it stimulates creativity and independence. Creating knitted fabric starts by casting the stitches on a knitting needle and continues by knitting with the other needle.

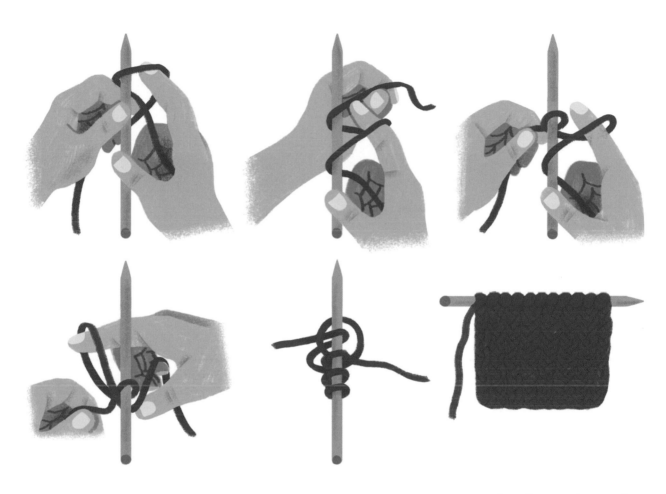

A FASHIONABLE HOBBY

Knitting is still fashionable today: it's relaxing and satisfying, and can be done anywhere. In recent years many people have started knitting clubs, organizing meetings where they can knit in the company of others or create group projects. And some of the most famous fashion designers in the world proudly create knitted and crocheted garments for the best fashion shows.

HOW WOOL IS WOVEN: THE LOOM

A popular way to use wool is by weaving. The lengthwise or vertical yarn, known as the warp, is crossed by the widthwise or horizontal yarn, known as the weft. The loom holds the warp stationary so that the weaver's hands can create a pattern with the weft.

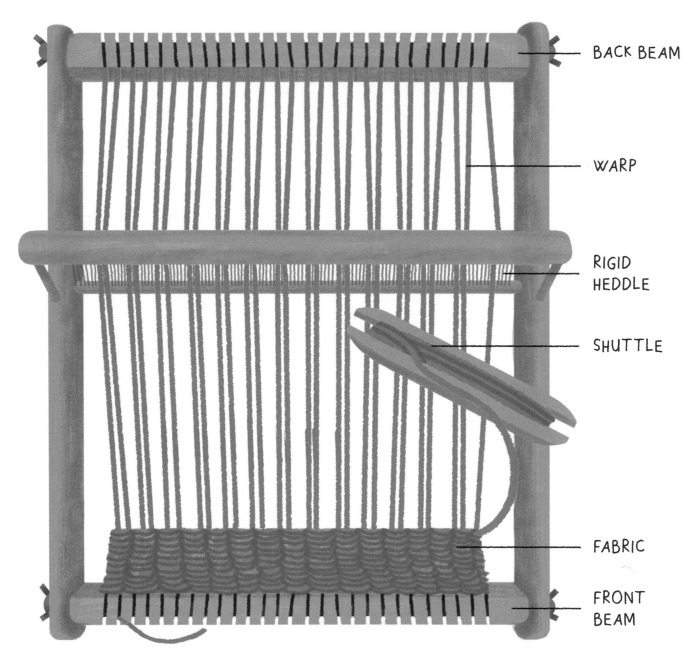

BACK BEAM

WARP

RIGID HEDDLE

SHUTTLE

FABRIC

FRONT BEAM

HOW A LOOM WORKS

The warp threads are strung tightly between two beams. In a simple loom, each warp thread passes through a rigid heddle, which lifts and lowers them, creating an opening for the shuttle with the weft thread to move horizontally through alternating warp threads. When the shuttle has passed all the way through, and the weft threads are slid into place, the shuttle can go back in the other direction. Each time the weft goes back and forth it adds to the length of the fabric, which forms on the front beam.

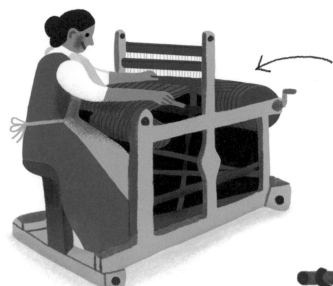

THE HORIZONTAL LOOM

The quickest way to weave is with a heddle loom, which was already being used by the Egyptians over 4,000 years ago and is still used today on an industrial scale. Even the simplest table looms, like the one on the previous page, follow the same principle.

THE VERTICAL LOOM

In the vertical loom, the warp threads hang from a horizontal bar and are held taut by weights tied to their free ends. This type of loom was used by many people throughout history, from the ancient Greeks to the Navajos and all around the world.

THE BACKSTRAP LOOM

In the backstrap loom, one bar is tied to a tree or other stationary device, while the second is attached to the weaver's waist. This ingenious method was once widespread across Asia and pre-Columbian Central and South America, and is still used in southern Mexico, Guatemala, and Peru.

POWER TO THE SHEEP

A PRECIOUS RESOURCE

In many parts of the world, and in different historical eras, owning sheep meant that you were rich. In ancient Rome, the name of the goddess Pecunia, the goddess of wealth, came from the word *pecus*, meaning livestock: a reminder that before money was invented to pay for things, sheep, chickens, and other animals were used instead. Sheep were also precious because of their wool, which was already being processed during the Iron Age, and the Romans used it to make togas.

YOUR SHEEP OR YOUR LIFE!

In the Middle Ages, wool became a well-developed industry, giving birth to one of the first major international trades. In England, half of the country's wealth depended on wool. When King Richard the Lionheart was taken hostage by Duke Leopold of Austria in 1192, his huge ransom was paid for, in part, thanks to wool. In practical terms, it is estimated that more than 10 million sheep paid out of their own pocket!

BUSINESS SHEEP

In the fifteenth century, the Flemish and Florentine weavers imported precious raw English wool to make Europe's most refined textiles. It was precisely because of this flourishing trade that the first banks were born, including that of the Medici, the most famous patrons of the Renaissance arts. If it weren't for sheep and their wool, we might not be able to admire the masterpieces of Michelangelo and Leonardo!

THE INDUSTRIAL REVOLUTION

Technology also transformed the wool industry: starting in the nineteenth century, work that was done by hand became mechanized, changing the way wool was manufactured, and by the late twentieth century the use of synthetic fibers, which cost less and are easier to wash, caused a crisis in the wool market.

A THREAD THAT COMES FROM AFAR

The history of humankind and that of wool are tied together by a double thread: spinning and weaving have strong symbolic meanings, and they are celebrated in many legends around the world. They have often been considered magical activities that already existed when the universe was born and were transmitted to humans by the deities.

THE GOLDEN FLEECE

In order to get his kingdom back from his evil uncle, Pelias, Jason had to bring him the famous golden fleece, protected by a ferocious dragon in faraway Colchis. The trip was long and difficult, but Jason was successful and brought back to Greece not only the fleece but Medea, too, the daughter of the King of Colchis. This myth may have originated from the practice of using sheep fleeces to sift gold dust suspended in the streams in a region that is now a part of Georgia.

THE GRANDMOTHER-SPIDER

For the Hopi, a Native tribe in the American Southwest, weaving is at the origins of the world: according to myth, at the dawn of time a grandmother-spider wove a strong and safe net where humans could live, sheltered from chaos and destruction. Other legends say that it was the grandmother-spider who taught humans the secrets of spinning and weaving.

LIFE HANGING FROM A THREAD

For thousands of years, spinning and weaving wool has been thought of as a woman's task. In Greek mythology, three goddesses known as the Fates controlled human destiny by assigning every human a personal thread: Clotho spun the thread, Lachesis measured it, and Atropos cut it off with her shears. Curiously, in Norse mythology, three women, known as the Norns, also spun human destinies.

FAIRY HANDS

In European folklore, every self-respecting fairy knows how to spin wool. In Russia, a household fairy named Domovika, who lived under the floorboards, would go out at night to spin, while in Germany the winter spirit Berchta is said to have developed a flat foot from the constant pounding on her spinning wheel. In Ireland and in Wales, a fairy spun and wove clothes for needy families.

DID SOMEONE MENTION SHEEP?

You likely know the Ben Franklin adage, "Make yourself a sheep and the wolves will eat you." There's a black sheep in every family. And who hasn't ever counted sheep to fall asleep? Our language is filled with sayings, expressions, and even superstitions related to sheep. Where do they come from?

BLACK SHEEP

SHEEP THAT COUNT

Sheep have always been so precious to humans that for every shepherd, counting them was the first thought in the morning and the last thought before falling asleep at night. To count them, some shepherds in England, Scotland, and Wales still use an ancient numerical system today known as Yan Tan Tethera. The only problem is that it only goes up to twenty, after which they have to start again from scratch. That can be a huge problem when you're dealing with a large flock!

THE BLACK SHEEP OF THE FAMILY

Over time, humans have selected sheep breeds to favor the ones with white wool, which is easier to dye. And yet a white sheep can still give birth to a black one. This phenomenon has led to numerous beliefs and superstitions. The idiom "the black sheep" is almost universal and is used to describe a person who is different from the other members of a family or group.

BORN UNDER THE SIGN OF THE SHEEP

Paradoxically, China, where there are more sheep than anywhere else in the world, has no idiom about black sheep. The sheep is one of the animals in the Chinese zodiac: people born under this sign are peace loving, gentle, and patient, but also shy and inclined to grumble. They are practically the opposite of the person who is an Aries, or a ram, in the Western zodiac: that person is considered stubborn, impulsive, and strong willed.

COUNTING SHEEP

Once upon a time the feudal lord Ezzelino III the Terrible hired a storyteller to entertain him when he couldn't sleep. One night, the storyteller, who was tired and wanted to sleep himself, told the lord a story about a flock crossing a river. The boatman ferried the first sheep to the other side, and then came back for the next one, and so on. At this point the storyteller stopped talking. When Ezzelino urged him to continue, he replied: "Sir, we need to get all the sheep to the other side first!" The storyteller was given permission to sleep.

CREATING A SMALL SHEEP FARM

You can decide to breed a small flock either out of passion or to produce milk, cheese, and wool for your own consumption. This hobby can be especially gratifying, but it also requires responsibility and consistency. This is why before getting any animals it's a good idea to spend some time at a farm that has sheep, to get used to them and figure out whether they're the right animal for you (and the other way around!).

Sheep are sociable animals, so a small flock should include at least four or five sheep, and, most importantly, there must be a suitable amount of land available.

One advantage to breeding sheep is that they can replace the lawn mower, cutting down lawns and pastures to perfection, and at the same time fertilizing them with excrement. Furthermore, sheep can keep the undergrowth clean, reducing the risk of fires.

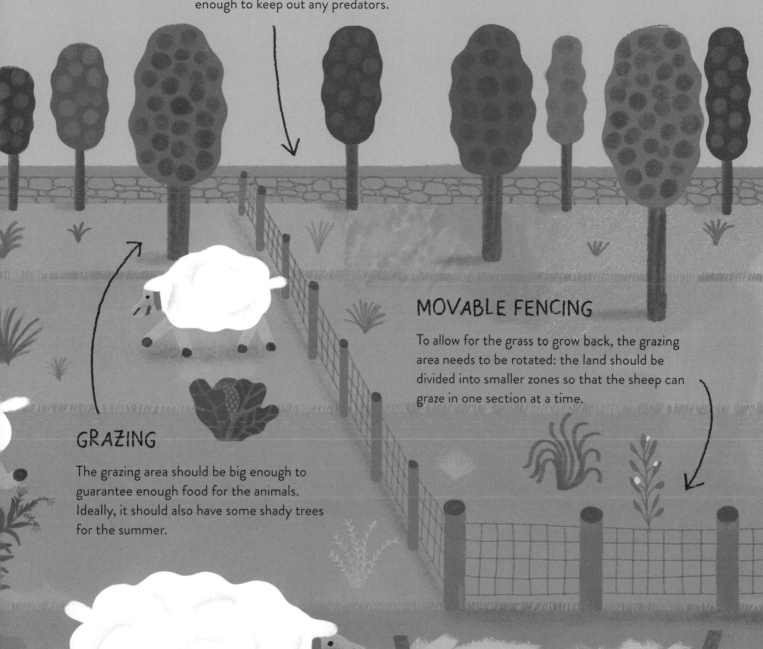

PERMANENT FENCING

The grazing area around the sheep pen must have a fence that's sturdy enough to keep out any predators.

MOVABLE FENCING

To allow for the grass to grow back, the grazing area needs to be rotated: the land should be divided into smaller zones so that the sheep can graze in one section at a time.

GRAZING

The grazing area should be big enough to guarantee enough food for the animals. Ideally, it should also have some shady trees for the summer.

HOME SWEET HOME: THE SHEEP PEN

Sheep aren't too demanding about their pen: all they need is a dry, covered, sheltered place where they can move around comfortably. Ideally, they should have around twenty square feet each. If they have a pasture, they will spend as little time as necessary in the sheep pen, only using it when the weather is bad or while giving birth.

In the winter season, when the sheep spend more time indoors and with their newborn lambs, the ground should be covered in straw to guarantee a warm, dry environment.

FEEDING TROUGH

Sheep eat grains or cereals from a trough.

HAYRACK
In the winter, the sheep eat hay directly from the hayrack.

WATER TROUGH

MAMA FARM

Tending to sheep means protecting them from predators, but also helping them when they are sick, providing medication, and asking for the help of a skilled veterinarian if necessary.

WHAT A SHEEP BREED!

Which sheep should you choose to start a farm? The mini-sheep,
known as Ouessants, or a soft Merino? A long-horned Racka
or a curly-haired Wensleydale? A Border Leicester with its ears
straight up like a rabbit, or a Bergamasca, whose ears are floppy?
It's hard to choose from the over one thousand breeds and
crossbreeds that are estimated to exist!

ZWARTBLES

LINCOLN

RACKA

OUESSANT

AN INTERNATIONAL FLOCK

Almost all the most popular breeds today come from England, from which they traveled with the colonists to the Americas and the Pacific. Because of both the crossbreeding performed by humans and the adaptation to various habitats the sheep had to undergo, over time the various breeds have succeeded in adjusting to every climate, from the torrid heat of the desert to the low temperatures of the highlands, developing different traits each time.

BETTER TO BE ALONE THAN IN BAD COMPANY

Some sheep breeds have remained undisturbed on far-flung islands or in remote Alpine villages, so they have never been crossbred with other sheep and have remained exactly the same as their ancestors. For instance, Soay sheep are the direct descendants of the first flock that arrived on the island of St Kilda thousands of years ago!

CALIFORNIA RED

WENSLEYDALE

BLUEFACED LEICESTER

SOAY

TEXEL

NORTH RONALDSAY

Origin	Orkney Island, Scotland
Fleece	Very thick, black and white, gray, light brown
Size	Very small
Weight	Rams 75 pounds, ewes 55 pounds

Notable features: If you go to North Ronaldsay, don't expect to see these sheep grazing in the meadow. They prefer the beach, where they live in the wild, feeding on the algae they absolutely love. They have a unique diet that has allowed them to survive in an extreme habitat, lulled by the sound of the tides: they sleep when the tide comes in and graze on the water's edge when the tide goes out.

Fun fact: This sheep's DNA is dated to 8,000 years ago, which likely makes it the most ancient ovine breed in northern Europe and among the oldest in the world. It has survived intact until the present time.

RED MAASAI

Origin	Kenya, Tanzania, and Uganda
Fleece	Ranges from red to brown
Size	Large and chunky
Weight	Rams 100 pounds, ewes 75 pounds

Notable features: This sheep, bred in the wild by the Maasai shepherds in the dry regions along the Great Rift Valley in southeast Africa, can survive long periods of drought. Instead of producing wool, it has thick red hair.

Fun fact: Livestock is important for the Maasai. Legend has it that the creator god, Enkai, sent the cattle sliding down a rope from the heavens into their safekeeping. The red sheep was the first animal to be bred by this community.

VAL SENALES

Origin   Italy

Fleece   Predominantly white

Size   Average

Weight   Rams 235 pounds, ewes 160 pounds

Notable features: Val Senales sheep have been living at high altitudes in the Alps for thousands of years and today continue to be bred by grazing alone.

Fun fact: Twice a year these sheep are taken from Val Senales, in Italy, to the Ötztal Valley, in Austria, for one of the few transhumances to cross a border between two countries. The trek is difficult, covering about 27 miles, with a 9,800-foot-altitude difference ascending, and a 5,900-foot-altitude difference descending. The journey ends with a great celebration in Italy in the fall.

VALAIS BLACKNOSE

Origin	Switzerland
Fleece	Black and white
Size	Average
Weight	Rams 175 pounds, ewes 155 pounds

Notable features: This very old breed inhabits the Swiss valleys, where it moves around with ease even on the steepest slopes.

Fun fact: This sheep is an influencer. Many believe it to be the prettiest sheep in the world, which is what makes it the most popular on social media, as well as celebrated by all the newspapers in the world. Unsurprisingly, it has millions of followers: besides being pretty, it is also very sociable and fun loving.

MERINO

Origin	Spain
Fleece	White
Size	Average
Weight	Rams 145–240 pounds, ewes 100–175 pounds

Notable features: The wool of the Merino is very fine, and the most suited of any wool to making fabrics. Believed to have come to Spain with the Moors, these sheep have conquered the world. The Australian variety has been the most successful, both because of the sheer number of animals and because of the quantity and quality of the wool.

Fun fact: Only the Spanish clergy and nobility were allowed to sell the fine Merino wool abroad—no other Spanish citizens were permitted. And exporting the sheep was prohibited, and even punishable by death!

AWASSI

Origin	Asia Minor and the Middle East
Fleece	White
Size	Large
Weight	Rams 200–265 pounds, ewes 145–175 pounds

Notable features: Among the hardiest sheep in the world, Awassis survive in dry climates thanks to the supply of fat stored in their tail and back. Their wool protects them from the heat by insulating them from the outside temperature, and when the sun is too hot, they hide their head in the shade, under the bellies of the other sheep.

Fun fact: This breed is suited to either sedentary or nomadic life. It can walk for miles on end: Awassis can walk an average of 4–5 miles, but if they need to find food and water, then they can even do 21 miles in just twenty-four hours!

SHROPSHIRE

Origin	Great Britain
Fleece	White
Size	Average
Weight	Rams 220–245 pounds, ewes 155–175 pounds

Notable features: Shropshire sheep are often put to pasture in the woods, vineyards, and orchards. They keep the undergrowth clean while fertilizing the plants.

Fun fact: One flock of Shropshire sheep had the honor of grazing the White House lawn. During World War I, these sheep not only mowed the grass free of charge for President Woodrow Wilson, but their wool was sold at auction, making $53,828 to fund the Red Cross. A patriotic sheep if there ever was one!

ICELANDIC

Origin	Iceland
Fleece	Varies from white to light brown to black
Size	Average
Weight	Rams 130–155 pounds, ewes 110–120 pounds

Notable features: Brought to Iceland 1,100 years ago by colonists, there are currently more sheep living on the island than people (400,000 versus around 366,000).

Fun fact: Icelandic sheep are allowed to graze freely in the highlands throughout the summer. In late August, the farmers climb up to fetch them along with all the other sheep they meet along the way, no matter whom the sheep belong to. Once they have been gathered in a large pen, they are sorted, each farmer grabbing his or her sheep by the horns.

ILARIA

Thanks to Debbie and Camilla for getting me involved in this baaaa-eautiful series. Thanks to the Rini family (especially Anna) and to their sheep (especially Tarzan) for the consulting, to Simone for his help, and to Brebis & Co. for their patience.

CAMILLA

To Elisa who, when she was a child, collected all the sheep she could find; to Giulia, my number one sponsor; to Margherita, who every year listens to stories about a different animal; to Marta, for all the files she had to convert in the final version; to Irene, who is patiently waiting for the book about ducks; and to my mother, who has become a great fan of this series!

Also by Camilla Pintonato from the same series
from Princeton Architectural Press

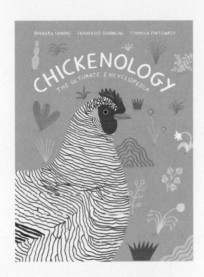